For information, address the publisher:
Raintree, 100 N. LaSalle, Suite 1200, Chicago, IL 60602

First published 2002
Under the title *Warrior 54: Confederate Cavalryman 1861–1865*
By Osprey Publishing Limited, Elms Court, Chapel Way, Botley, Oxford, OX2 9LP
© 2002 Osprey Publishing Limited
All rights reserved.

ISBN 1-4109-0114-9

03 04 05 06 07   10 9 8 7 6 5 4 3 2 1

Library of Congress Cataloging-in-Publication Data

Katcher, Philip R. N.
   [Confederate cavalryman, 1861-65]
   Confederate cavalrymen of the Civil War / Philip Katcher.
       v. cm. -- (A soldier's life)
Originally published: Confederate cavalryman, 1861-65. Oxford [England] : Osprey, 2002, in series: Warrior.
Includes bibliographical references and index.
Contents: Regular cavalry -- Recruiting -- Training, uniforms, equipment, and weapons -- Everyday life -- Campaign life -- Battle -- Partisan rangers -- Scouts and couriers.
   ISBN 1-4109-0114-9 (lib. bdg.)
   1. Confederate States of America. Army. Cavalry--History--Juvenile literature. 2. Soldiers--Confederate States of America--History--Juvenile literature. 3. United States--History--Civil War, 1861-1865--Cavalry operations--Juvenile literature. [1. Confederate States of America. Army. Cavalry--History. 2. Soldiers--Confederate States of America--History. 3. United States--History--Civil War, 1861-1865--Cavalry operations.] I. Title. II. Series.
   E546.5.K38 2003
   973.7'42--dc21
                        2003005280

Author: Philip Katcher
Illustrator: Gerry Embleton
Editor: Thomas Lowres
Design: Ken Vail Graphic Design, Cambridge, UK
Index by Alan Rutter
Originated by Magnet Harlequin, Uxbridge, UK
Printed in China through World Print Ltd.

Artist's note

Readers may care to note that the original paintings from which the color plates in this book were prepared are available for private sale. All reproduction copyright whatsoever is retained by the Publishers. All enquiries should be addressed to:

Scorpio Gallery
PO Box 475
Hailsham
E Sussex
BN27 2SL

Acknowledgments

All illustrations are author's own collection unless otherwise indicated.